THE BOOK OF
UNITED STATES NAVY SHIPS

THE BOOK OF
UNITED STATES NAVY SHIPS

By M. D. Van Orden
REAR ADMIRAL, U.S. NAVY (RETIRED)

ILLUSTRATED WITH PHOTOGRAPHS

FOURTH EDITION, FULLY REVISED

DODD, MEAD & COMPANY · NEW YORK

All photographs are official U.S. Navy photographs.

Library of Congress Cataloging in Publication Data

Van Orden, M. D., date
The book of United States Navy ships.

Includes index.
Summary: Text and photographs introduce the
characteristics and purposes of the various types of ships
in the present-day Navy.
1. United States. Navy—Juvenile literature.
2. Warships—United States—Juvenile literature.
[1. United States. Navy. 2. Warships. 3. Ships]
I. Title.
VA58.4.V36   1985   359.8'3   84-24640
ISBN 0-396-08543-1

To the dedicated, competent, and patriotic men and women
who serve in the ships of the U.S. Navy

PREFACE

A modern Navy is many things—ships, boats, aircraft, men, women, guns, missiles, shore bases, and equipment of all types—but the heart of any Navy is its ships.

Ships are built to many different designs, depending upon what they will be required to do. There may be a number of different types, classes, conversions, and modifications of each basic design. Changes become necessary; consequently, improvements in designs are made. Major changes are required to adapt to new techniques of warfare or to new technological advances. For example, the changes from sail to steam; the transition from wooden hulls to steel; the advent of nuclear propulsion systems; the shift from guns to missiles; the introduction of radar, sonar, and modern communications—all of these advances have resulted in radical changes in ship designs.

The purpose of this book is to illustrate and explain the most important and most representative types and classes of ships in today's United States Navy, and to describe some of their characteristics. In addition, it will discuss the part each ship plays—its "mission"—as a member of the Navy teams—the "Fleets" and "Battle Groups" of the modern U.S. Navy.

Upon these ships and these well-trained teams rest our country's power, prestige, and safety. A strong Navy of capable, modern, well-equipped, well-manned ships can do much to discourage aggression and preserve the peace.

Washington, D.C.

M. D. Van Orden
Rear Admiral, U.S. Navy (Retired)

Now these are the laws of the Navy,
    Unwritten and varied they be;
And he that is wise will observe them,
    Going down in his ship to the sea;
As naught may outrun the destroyer,
    Even so with the law in its grip,
For the strength of the ship is the Service,
    And the strength of the Service, the ship.

from *The Laws of the Navy,*
by Captain Ronald A. Hopwood, R.N.

CONTENTS

Surface view, bow on, of the U.S.S. *Permit* **(SSN-594).**

NAVY TERMINOLOGY

When Navymen talk of their ships, they use words and phrases which may seem strange to those who are not acquainted with the ways of the sea. Yet to seamen those words and phrases have meanings which are well known and precise. They have been developed over many years by seafaring men who chose carefully those expressions which would not be misunderstood by other seamen—even during the stresses of battles or raging storms. Many expressions used today are only representative of past traditions of the sea, yet they are cherished and perpetuated by men who are bound together by their common heritage of service at sea.

Ships are always referred to as "she." There have been many reasons given for this. Some think it is because of the feminine beauty a sailor sees in his ship; others say it is because of the difficulty men have in understanding, directing, and controlling "her." Perhaps the ancient Greeks started the custom by giving their ships female names to honor Athena, the goddess of warships. Whatever the reason, a sailor always thinks and speaks of his ship as a "she," never an "it."

Navymen always go "on board" a ship, or "in" a ship—never "on" a ship. A favorite saying is, "Seamen go down to the seas *in* ships; landlubbers go to sea *on* ships."

Don't make the mistake around sailormen of calling a ship a boat. A tourist aboard a cruise ship such as the *Queen Elizabeth* brings forth only disgust among seamen by saying, "My boat sails at 8 o'clock." What is the difference between ships and boats? It is largely a matter of size, with the smaller craft being recognized as boats. A salty old Chief Petty Officer with many years of seagoing experience once stated it simply to a group of Midshipmen, saying, "A boat is any craft that can be hoisted aboard a ship—and don't you forget it!" There is one exception allowed: submarine sailors call their submarines "boats" despite the fact that by size alone they are classed as ships. Probably this custom dates from the early days when the subs were known as "pigboats" because of their resemblance in shape and color to young porkers, and because of the way they clustered around their "mother" ships when in harbor.

Most people are aware of the use of "port" and "starboard" to mean the left and right sides of a ship when facing forward. Also "fore" and "after" to mean the front and rear of a ship, and "forward" and "aft"

The helmsman on the bridge of U.S.S. *Spruance* (DD-963)

Opposite: The superstructure is that part of a ship built above the main deck and used for living or working spaces.

to indicate "toward the front" and "toward the rear." The "bow" is the most forward part of the ship, and the "stern" the after part. The length of a ship is the distance from bow to stern, the width from side to side is called the "beam," and the "draft" is the vertical distance from the waterline to the deepest part of the hull.

Almost everyone knows that aboard ship the floors are called "decks," the ceilings are called "overheads," the walls are known as "bulkheads," and the stairs are known as "ladders." When a sailor goes up a ladder to or above the "main" deck (the uppermost deck which extends from bow to stern), he will say, "I'm going topside"; when going back down into the ship, he says, "I'm going below." These are the equivalent of upstairs and downstairs to people who are not accustomed to living in ships.

An aircraft carrier's superstructure above the flight deck is called the island. U.S.S. *Constellation* (CV-64).

A ship's "superstructure" is that portion of the ship built above the main deck and used for living or working spaces. In an aircraft carrier the superstructure above the "flight" deck (that deck used for aircraft landings and takeoffs) is called the "island." The "bridge" of a ship, located in the superstructure or island, is that location where the ship is "conned" or controlled by the Captain and his officers.

When a ship is "underway" (floating free—not attached to a land structure such as a pier, and not having an anchor on the bottom), she is driven through the water by "screws," as the propellers are called.

The screws are large, pusher-type propellers that operate under water at relatively slow speeds—slow, that is, when compared with the puller-type propellers one sees on some airplanes. The screws push the ship through the water at speeds which are measured in "knots." A knot is a measure of speed—not distance. It is a speed of one nautical mile per hour; a nautical mile is 6,080 feet, slightly longer than a mile on land, because of its derivation by early navigators from geographic measures—i.e., one nautical mile equals one minute of latitude.

The speed of a ship through the water for a given speed of rotation of her screws depends upon a number of factors: her condition of loading (she may be expected to move more slowly when heavily loaded than when empty), the resistance or push exerted on her superstructure and hull by high winds, the state of the sea (high waves may slow her down or may even at times expose her screws, causing loss of propulsion efficiency), and the condition of her bottom (growth of weeds or barnacles slow her down). Nevertheless, each ship has a "rated speed" at which she is expected to travel at each speed of rotation of her screws. This is the speed expected under normal conditions for each hull type, and is usually established by "speed trials" when the ship is new. The expression "rated speed" refers to the maximum speed at which the ship can conduct sustained operations.

Another nautical term, "displacement," is of interest. The weight of a ship is equal to the weight of the volume of water which she occupies (displaces) when afloat. When speaking of the weight of his ship, a Navy man will say, "She displaces 40,000 tons," or "Her full load displacement is 40,000 tons."

Ships are organized into "Fleets" and "Battle Groups" for operational control and for coordinated performance of their assigned missions. A Fleet is a large number of ships of different types placed under the operational control of a fleet commander, such as "Commander, Third Fleet." A Battle Group is a smaller grouping of different types of ships which are selected to accomplish a specific task, or tasks. For example, a "Carrier Battle Group" includes the aircraft carriers to conduct air operations against an enemy, the cruisers to provide gun and missile protection against enemy ships and aircraft, and the escorting destroyers and frigates to provide protection against enemy submarines. These are the Navy "teams" which join together ships of different types to accomplish assigned missions as cohesive units.

All of these expressions are used by men of the sea when speaking of ships.

SHIP NAMES

Navy ships have names that contain a great deal of information about the ship. There are four parts to a name—for example, consider the U.S.S. *Enterprise* (CVN-65).

The first part, U.S.S., stands for United States Ship and is a part of the name of every *commissioned* ship in the U.S. Navy—that is, every ship that has been officially commissioned as a member of our Navy.

The second part, *Enterprise*, is the actual name. Names are assigned by rules which will be explained later. Since *Enterprise* is the name which was formerly carried by a number of famous ships in our history, those who are familiar with Navy history and traditions know that it now indicates an aircraft carrier.

The third part of the name, CVN, tells what type of ship this is. CV is the Navy designation for aircraft carriers, and the N denotes a ship having nuclear propulsion.

Finally, the fourth part of the name, 65, is the "hull number." Hull numbers are normally assigned in sequence for each type of ship; so 65 means that *Enterprise* is the 65th aircraft carrier commissioned in the U.S. Navy. This number is also the number painted on the ship's bow (and the island and flight deck of an aircraft carrier), and so is sometimes called the "bow number" as well.

Thus, by the name U.S.S. *Enterprise* (CVN-65), we know that this is a commissioned ship of the U.S. Navy, named *Enterprise* (after one or more famous Navy ships of the past), that she is a nuclear-powered aircraft carrier, and is the 65th carrier on the Navy rolls.

Each ship of the Navy may be identified in similar fashion—by one who knows the meanings of the ship names and designators.

The island of the U.S.S. *Enterprise* (CVN-65). The hull number on the island can be seen clearly.

HOW SHIPS ARE NAMED

Ships of the U.S. Navy are named by the Secretary of the Navy in accordance with traditional rules and customs. In 1819, the Congress decided that "ships of the first class" would be named for states of the United States, those of the second class for rivers, and third-class ships would be named to honor U.S. cities.Later, in 1858, the rules were relaxed and Congress allowed names to be assigned "by the Secretary of the Navy as the President shall direct." Until after World War II, submarines were named for fish, battleships for states, cruisers for cities, aircraft carriers for famous battles and earlier ships, and destroyers for dead Navy and Marine Corps heroes. These rules are not always followed today.

AIRCRAFT CARRIERS are named after famous ships formerly on the Navy list (U.S.S. *Constellation*), or for important battles (U.S.S. *Midway*). In recent years, carriers have been named to honor Presidents and famous leaders of the United States (U.S.S. *John F. Kennedy,* U.S.S. *Forrestal*).

BATTLESHIPS are named for states (U.S.S. *Missouri,* U.S.S. *New Jersey*). Since so few battleships remain, other capital ships are now also given the names of states (U.S.S. *Ohio,* a Trident submarine, and U.S.S. *Virginia,* a cruiser, are examples).

CRUISERS were formerly named for cities; however, only the U.S.S. *Long Beach* still carries that designation. In 1975, ships of large destroyer types were reclassified as cruisers; these continue to carry their same names—those assigned originally as destroyer names (U.S.S. *Leahy*). Guided-missile, nuclear-propelled cruisers are now being named for states (U.S.S. *Texas*).

DESTROYERS and FRIGATES are named to honor deceased heroes of the Navy, Marine Corps, and Coast Guard (U.S.S. *Spruance,* U.S.S. *Valdez*). They may also be named for members of Congress and for Secretaries and Assistant Secretaries of the Navy.

BALLISTIC MISSILE SUBMARINES are named in honor of distinguished Americans (U.S.S. *Thomas A. Edison,* U.S.S. *Sam Houston*). The very large (Trident missile design) ballistic missile submarines are named after states (U.S.S. *Ohio,* U.S.S. *Michigan*).

SUBMARINES are named after fish and other sea creatures (U.S.S. *Haddock,* U.S.S. *Seahorse*). Some are named to honor members of Congress; the newest classes are being named after cities (U.S.S. *Los Angeles*).

Crewmen man their duty stations in the Combat Information Center of the destroyer U.S.S. *Spruance* (DD-963).

SHIP TYPES AND DESIGNATIONS

Ships of different types are given different letter designations. Although there is no exact meaning in the letters assigned, most of them were developed in a logical manner. For example, auxiliary ships have designators beginning with the letter "A." "AD," the designation for Destroyer Tenders, could be interpreted as "Auxiliary Ship for Destroyers." Ships with "L" as the first letter in their designations are generally those used in amphibious warfare (Landing Ships). BB denotes Battleships, DD indicates Destroyers, SS identifies submarines, FF is the designator for Frigates, the first letter C stands for Cruiser, and CV for Carrier of heavier-than-air aircraft.

There are a few special letters that are used as part of the designation of all types of ships: "E" before the designator means that the ship is Experimental, "G" after a designator indicates that the ship is equipped with Guided Missiles, and the letter "N" after the designator denotes a ship with nuclear power.

Left: Cooks of the U.S.S. *Coral Sea* (CVA-43) standing by one of the two serving lines of the after mess deck.

Opposite: Crew having noon meal aboard the U.S.S. *Nimitz* (CVN-68).

Although ship *types* are clearly identified by letter designations, the letters do not show which *class* the ship belongs to. The type refers to the basic category of ship, such as Battleship (type BB), Submarine (type SS), Destroyer (type DD), and the like. However, within each *type* of ship there may be a number of different classes. This happens because over a period of years one or more ships of the same type may be built to essentially the same set of plans (same class)—they are similar in length, beam, displacement, and general arrangement—while others of the same type may be built to a different design and thereby become a different class. Thus a destroyer is given an individual name and each also has a class designation. She may be one of any of several destroyer classes, such as the *Spruance* (DD-963) class or of the *Farragut*

(DDG-37) class, meaning that she is similar to the other ships of that particular "model" or class. For example, U.S.S. *Arthur W. Radford* (DD-968) is a *Spruance* class destroyer.

The classes are named after the first ship of the new design commissioned, and usually the ships in that class have hull numbers in sequence immediately following the first ship of the class. How many ships are in each class depends upon the shipbuilding program in effect while that particular design is considered to be the best available—that is, until some new design or model is approved for building and a new class started.

There are many different ship types in the U.S. Navy, each with a different designation. Each type may contain a number of different classes, but the class cannot be determined from the letter designation. Listed on the following page are the most common or most representative types of ships and their assigned letter designations.

DESIG-NATION	TYPE OF SHIP	DESIG-NATION	TYPE OF SHIP
AD	Destroyer Tender	DDG	Guided Missile Destroyer
AE	Ammunition Ship	FF	Frigate (Former DE)
AFS	Combat Store Ship	FFG	Guided Missile Frigate
AO	Oiler	LCC	Amphibious Command Ship
AOE	Fast Combat Support Ship	LHA	Amphibious Assault Ship
AOR	Replenishment Oiler	LKA	Amphibious Cargo Ship
AR	Repair Ship	LPD	Amphibious Transport, Dock
ARS	Salvage Ship	LPH	Amphibious Assault Ship
AS	Submarine Tender	LSD	Landing Ship, Dock
ASR	Submarine Rescue Ship	LST	Landing Ship, Tank
ATF	Fleet Ocean Tug	MSO	Minesweeper, Ocean
ATS	Salvage Tug	PG	Patrol Gunboat
BB	Battleship	PHM	Patrol, Hydrofoil, (Missile)
CG	Guided Missile Cruiser	SS	Submarine
CGN	Guided Missile Cruiser (Nuclear Powered)	SSBN	Ballistic Missile Submarine (Nuclear Powered)
CV	Aircraft Carrier		
CVN	Aircraft Carrier (Nuclear Powered)	SSN	Submarine (Nuclear Powered)
DD	Destroyer		

Part 1 — AIRCRAFT CARRIERS

The Aircraft Carrier is the most important member of the modern Navy team and the backbone of today's powerful Battle Groups. It is the first new type of warship produced in this century; its introduction revolutionized naval warfare. Today the aircraft carrier is the principal surface ship through which our use of the seas in support of national objectives is assured.

A carrier is a mobile air base which can operate in international waters on all parts of the globe, and with great speed and power be on the scene and in action rapidly whenever needed. The carrier's mission is to use her aircraft to control the air around and above the operating area, denying to any enemy the advantage of having free access to that area. With squadrons of fighter, bomber, and reconnaissance aircraft aboard, the carrier provides close air support for troops ashore, protection of friendly ships and boats, and reconnaissance information on enemy movements and installations. The reconnaissance aircraft also provide detection and constant surveillance of all submarines and surface ships over a wide area, calling on attack aircraft where necessary to protect our forces. Thus, a carrier Battle Group can apply the precise force required in any situation, and provide strong support whenever trouble arises.

The most modern carriers are the nuclear-powered type—that is, those having nuclear reactors as the heart of their main propulsion machinery. Using a controlled nuclear reaction instead of an oil-fired boiler to generate heat which produces steam to drive the turbines, they have a long-lasting, instantly available source of power. Increased aviation fuel and aviation ordnance capacity is possible because a nuclear-powered carrier does not need to devote space in its hull to carrying a supply of propulsion fuel oil. The Navy has four nuclear carriers in service today and two additional are planned for future service.

With their need of response and their high degree of logistic independence, these nuclear-powered carriers are the heart of the Navy's quick reaction forces for the next decade. They are able to move rapidly to areas of potential crisis without delaying for logistic support forces carrying fuel oil, to conduct protective air operations en route, and then to carry out sustained air operations in their assigned operating areas. These carriers represent a national capability to bring to bear effective military strength in distant areas with closely controlled, versatile forces.

U.S.S. Nimitz

U.S.S. NIMITZ (CVN-68)   *Nimitz* is the lead ship of a new class of very large, nuclear-powered aircraft carriers. These are the largest, most powerful warships in the world. They are 1,092 feet long, have a beam of 252 feet at the widest point of the flight deck, can accommodate a crew of 6,286 officers and men, and their combat load displacement is 95,000 tons. *Nimitz* class carriers have two reactors and nuclear fuel for 13 years of normal carrier operations, the equivalent of 11 million barrels of propulsion fuel oil. With a rated speed in excess of 30 knots, these ships can support a modern air wing of about 100 planes. Other active ships of the *Nimitz* class are U.S.S. *Dwight D. Eisenhower* (CVN-69), U.S.S. *Carl Vinson* (CVN-70), and U.S.S. *Theodore Roosevelt* (CVN-71). Two additional ships of this class are planned for delivery in future years.

U.S.S. ENTERPRISE (CVN-65)   *Enterprise* is the first nuclear-powered aircraft carrier ever built. She was commissioned in November, 1961, and has since made a number of remarkable records. In 1964, *Enterprise*, with Nuclear Task Force One, circumnavigated the world—cruising over 30,000 miles without taking on fuel or provisions. Theoretically she could cruise eight times around the globe without need to renew her nuclear fuel. She is 1,123 feet in length, with a maximum beam (flight deck) of 257 feet and a maximum draft of 37 feet. Her flight deck has an area of about 4½ acres—three football fields could be placed on the flight deck area. Main engines generate up to 360,000 horsepower, which will drive her at speeds of over 30 knots. She has a crew of more than 4,000 and normally carries about 90 aircraft. Full load displacement is 86,000 tons.

U.S.S. JOHN F. KENNEDY (CV-67)   The only ship of her class, *Kennedy* was commissioned in 1968 as an improved version of the *Kitty Hawk* class. She displaces 87,000 tons, has a length of 1,047½ feet and a beam of 252 feet. The latest and possibly last of the non-nuclear powered carriers, she has 8 boilers which can generate 280,000 horsepower to produce a rated speed in excess of 30 knots.

U.S.S. *Enterprise*

U.S.S. *John F. Kennedy*

U.S.S. KITTY HAWK (CV-63)   Commissioned in April, 1961, she is the first of three modern large carriers in the *Kitty Hawk* class. Others in this class are U.S.S. *Constellation* (CV-64) and U.S.S. *America* (CV-66). These ships are 1,047½ feet long, with a maximum beam of 252 feet and a 37-foot maximum draft. Main engines capable of generating 280,000 horsepower give them a rated speed of 34 knots. Each carries a crew of over 4,000 and has more than 70 aircraft. Full load displacement is 78,000 tons.

U.S.S. FORRESTAL (CV-59)   Commissioned in October, 1955, *Forrestal* is the lead ship in a four-ship class, including U.S.S. *Saratoga* (CV-60), U.S.S. *Ranger* (CV-61), and U.S.S. *Independence* (CV-

U.S.S. *Kitty Hawk*

62). *Forrestal* has a length overall of 1,039 feet, while the other three are 1,046 feet overall. *Forrestal's* full load displacement is 76,000 tons; that of the other class ships is 78,700 tons. In other respects they are the same: beam is 252 feet, draft is 37 feet, and all carry more than 70 aircraft and a crew of over 4,000 officers and men. *Forrestal* has slightly less power in her main engines (260,000 horsepower), giving a rated speed of 33 knots. The other three ships have main engines of 280,000 horsepower, and rated speed of 34 knots.

U.S.S. MIDWAY (CV-41)

First commissioned in 1945, just after World War II, *Midway* is the leader of the first class of "Big Carriers" which the Navy looked toward in the postwar years. Others in the class are U.S.S. *Franklin D. Roosevelt* (CV-42) and U.S.S. *Coral Sea* (CV-43). These ships are 979 feet long, with a maximum beam of 222 feet, and a maximum draft of 36 feet. They have a rated speed of 33 knots, carry 70 or more aircraft, and have a crew of over 4,000. Full load displacement is 62,000 tons. *Coral Sea* displaces 63,600 tons. All three ships were completely overhauled and modernized in the middle 1950's, and continue to perform well.

U.S.S. *Forrestal*

U.S.S. *Midway*

Part 2 — BATTLESHIPS AND CRUISERS

Battleships and Cruisers are designed to be able to fight battles at sea against enemy ships, using their guns, missiles, and armor plate to best advantage. Unlike the carriers which must rely on their aircraft for their primary protection, the battleships and cruisers protect themselves with their own guns and missiles. They may be equipped with surface-to-surface missiles as well as anti-aircraft missiles, and thus are able to fire beyond the range of their guns by a considerable amount. Their mission is to engage enemy ships with gun and missile fire, to deliver heavy and continuous bombardment against enemy shore installations, and to provide protection to their Battle Group against enemy aircraft. In addition, they frequently serve as flagships and carry both the staff and the communications equipment necessary for the conduct of at-sea operations of Battle Groups.

The former designations of ''Heavy Cruiser'' (CA) and ''Light Cruiser'' (CL), which referred to the size of the main battery guns installed, are no longer in use, since all cruisers today have missile batteries as their main armament instead of guns. The cruisers in today's Navy include those classes formerly known as ''Destroyer Leaders'' or ''Guided Missile Frigates'' (DL, DLG, and DLGN), which are similar in size to earlier cruisers and have been redesignated as CG and CGN.

In recent years, the need for heavy gunfire support of forces ashore has prompted the recall to active duty of the Navy's remaining World War II battleships. In addition to their powerful sixteen-inch guns, these large, heavily armored ships are ideal for directing combat operations and for providing the necessary storage space and stable platform for launching a variety of missiles.

U.S.S. NEW JERSEY (BB-62)   This is one of four *Iowa* class battleships decommissioned and placed ''in mothballs'' after World War II. She has been recommissioned three times—to support forces in Korea and Vietnam, and most recently to play a major role in future U.S. Naval operations. Her first combat performance after the third reactivation was to support the U.S. Marines ashore in Lebanon. The other three *Iowa* class battleships are the U.S.S. *Iowa* (BB-61), the U.S.S. *Missouri* (BB-63), and the U.S.S. *Wisconsin* (BB-64). All four are 887 feet in length, with a beam of 108 feet, and a draft of 38 feet

U.S.S. New Jersey

U.S.S. *Virginia*

maximum. Displacement is 59,300 tons, and the full wartime crew is 2,700 officers and men. Their main engines generate 212,000 horsepower, driving the ships with a rated speed of 31 knots. With nine 16-inch guns, each capable of hurling 2,700-pound projectiles more than 20 miles with pinpoint precision, these ships are able to give strong gunfire support to our forces operating against an enemy. Their steel armor plate (16 inches thick on turrets and conning tower, 12 inches thick along her sides, and 5 inches thick on her armor deck) provides protection to vital spaces against all but the largest bombs, missiles, and projectiles.

U.S.S. VIRGINIA (CGN-38)   The lead ship of a new class of eight nuclear-powered guided-missile cruisers, *Virginia* is 585 feet in length, with a beam of 63 feet. She displaces 11,000 tons and is manned by 38 officers and 459 enlisted men. These ships are powered by two nuclear reactors which give a speed of over 30 knots. Their armament consists of Tartar missiles, anti-submarine rockets (ASROC), two 5-inch/54 caliber lightweight guns, two torpedo launchers, and a helicopter. Other ships of the class are U.S.S. *Texas* (CGN-39), U.S.S. *Mississippi* (CGN-40, U.S.S. *Arkansas* (CGN-41), and the as yet unnamed CGNs 42, 43, 44, and 45.

U.S.S. *California*

U.S.S. *Bainbridge*

U.S.S. CALIFORNIA (CGN-36)   There are two ships in this class, the other being the U.S.S. *South Carolina* (CGN-37). Both are missile cruisers, equipped with dual Tartar launchers fore and aft; both also have a single 5-inch/54 gun forward and aft. They are 596 feet in length, with a beam of 61 feet and a draft of 31½ feet. Powered by nuclear reactors, they are rated at speeds in excess of 30 knots. Their displacement is 11,000 tons.

U.S.S. BAINBRIDGE (CGN-25) and U.S.S. TRUXTUN (CGN-35)   Each of these ships is a single ship class of approximately the same design. Both were former DLGNs (frigates), having been reclassified as CGNs in 1975. *Bainbridge*, commissioned in 1966, was the first nuclear-powered frigate and *Truxtun* the second, commissioned in 1966. *Bainbridge* displaces 8,700 tons, is 564 feet long, with a beam of 58 feet and maximum draft of 24½ feet. Her two nuclear reactors generate more than 60,000 horsepower to drive her at speeds greater than 30 knots. Her armament consists of four 3-inch guns, two twin Terrier missile launchers, and an ASROC (Anti-Submarine Rocket) launcher. Her crew numbers 400 officers and men. She participated in the circumnavigation of the globe in 1964 with Nuclear Task Force One, cruising 30,216 nautical miles without taking on fuel or provisions. *Truxtun* is about the same dimensions, but with a draft of 30 feet and displacement of 9,050 tons. She carries one twin Terrier launcher, one 5-inch gun, and DASH (Drone Anti-Submarine Helicopter) for conducting ASW operations with a "drone" (remote-controlled, unmanned) helicopter.

U.S.S. JOSEPHUS DANIELS (CG-27)   This is the second ship of the *Belknap* class of nine former DLGs, now reclassified as CGs. They are designed to screen carrier Battle Groups. Equipped with both missile and anti-

U.S.S. *Josephus Daniels*

submarine rocket launchers, they are excellent for operations against aircraft and submarines. Displacement is 7,900 tons, length is 547 feet, beam is 55 feet, and the four-boiler, steam-turbine main power plant generates 60,000 shaft horsepower, capable of producing speeds above 32 knots.

U.S.S. LEAHY (CG-16)

There are nine ships in the *Leahy* class. They are equipped with anti-aircraft missile launchers on the fore and after decks, as well as an anti-submarine rocket launcher mounted forward. They are designed to screen carrier Battle Groups. Displacing 7,800 tons, they are 533 feet in length, with a beam of 55 feet, and draft of 25 feet. A main power plant of four boilers and steam turbines generates 85,000 shaft horsepower and a speed in excess of 32 knots.

U.S.S. *Leahy*

U.S.S. Long Beach

U.S.S. *Ticonderoga*

U.S.S. LONG BEACH (CGN-9)　　The Navy's first nuclear-powered surface ship, the guided missile cruiser *Long Beach* was commissioned in September, 1961. Her main battery consists of Surface-to-Air Missiles (SAMs)—two Terrier twin launchers forward and a single Talos twin launcher aft. Twin nuclear reactors generate steam to drive *Long Beach* at speeds in excess of 30 knots, and during Operation Sea Orbit, as a member of Nuclear Task Force One, she traveled around the world without taking on fuel or provisions. Her overall length is 721 feet, her beam is 73 feet, and her maximum draft is 26 feet. Full load displacement is 16,250 tons. Her large, boxlike superstructure is an oddity among cruisers. It, like the island of *Enterprise*, carries large radar antennas on each of the flat faces of the structure.

U.S.S. TICONDEROGA (CG-47)　　This is a new class of *Aegis* ships—so-called because they have been modified to carry the Aegis fire control system, a very complex, computer-controlled radar and missile system designed to provide the finest available anti-aircraft protection. The *Ticonderoga* class design is a modification of the *Spruance* class ships, and plans are for a total of 22 of these very capable, non-nuclear cruisers. *Ticonderoga* was commissioned in 1983; the second ship of the class, U.S.S. *Yorktown* (CG-48), and the following 20 ships are planned later additions to the Fleet. The ships of this class have a full load displacement of 9,200 tons. In all other respects, their characteristics are similar to those of the *Spruance* class.

Part 3 — DESTROYERS AND FRIGATES

The destroyer types are the most versatile of our Navy's warships. Their duties include bombarding enemy shore installations, blockading shipping, escorting Navy task forces and merchant ship convoys, and providing vital defense against enemy submarines and aircraft. Essentially lightly constructed, fast, highly maneuverable ships, the "tin cans" (so-called because of their thin steel, unarmored hulls) depend upon speed and firepower rather than on armor for protection.

Frigates are a recent addition to the fleet. In post-World War II days, the Destroyer Leaders (DL) were called Frigates. When, in 1975, the larger ones were reclassified as Cruisers and the smaller as Destroyers, the name Frigate was given to the existing Destroyer Escort (DE) classes.

The missions of the Frigate and Destroyer are many. They provide gunfire and missile support to forces afloat and ashore, and their speed and maneuverability make them excellent patrol and intercept ships to prevent enemy ships from entering protected zones. (The name "destroyer" evolved from their first use, that of "torpedo boat destroyer.") They are also excellent air defense ships; with their missiles and dual-purpose guns they can be employed against either surface targets or air targets. One important mission is providing protection against enemy submarines. All are equipped with SONAR (SOund Navigation And Ranging) equipment for detecting and tracking submerged submarines and a number of weapons for attacking enemy submarines detected. Their speed and maneuverability make them excellent ships for detecting, tracking, and destroying enemy submarines. Finally, their mission includes the use of their torpedoes against enemy ships if such attacks become possible.

With such a versatile ship, the Navy needs are for large numbers both in peacetime and wartime. The U.S. Navy has well over a hundred in commission, made up of many different classes of Destroyers and Frigates. The newer classes of both are equipped with modern missiles, electronics equipments, and other advanced technology devices needed for proper performance of their many missions.

U.S.S. FARRAGUT (DDG-37)

Originally a DL (DLG-6), *Farragut* is the lead ship of ten DDGs of a class commissioned between 1959 and 1961. DDG-37 through 46 are "single enders" (guided missiles

U.S.S. *Farragut*

U.S.S. Charles F. Adams

either forward or aft—not both) with a 5-inch gun forward and a twin Terrier missile launcher aft. Full load displacement is 5,350 tons. Length is 512½ feet, beam is 52½ feet, and maximum draft is 25 feet. With 4 boilers generating 85,000 horsepower, their rated speed is 34 knots.

U.S.S. CHARLES F. ADAMS (DDG-2) The first of 23 general-purpose Anti-Air Warfare/Anti-Submarine Warfare (AAW/ASW) destroyers, *Adams* was commissioned in September, 1960. Although the basic hull design is the same for all of the *Adams* class (DDG-2 through 24), there are differences in

U.S.S. *Spruance*

armament and detection equipment carried. Their major characteristics are: Length, 432 feet; beam, 47 feet; maximum draft, 20 feet; and displacement 4,500 tons. Their 80,000 horsepower engines drive them at a rated speed of 35 knots. Each crew numbers 354 officers and men. Basic armament for the class is two single-mount 5-inch guns, one forward and one aft, an ASROC installation amidships, and a twin Tartar guided missile launcher aft.

U.S.S. SPRUANCE (DD-963)

Spruance is the lead ship of a completely new design class of 30 destroyers, planned to replace older DD classes in the fleet. The ships are designed primarily for the anti-submarine warfare mission, and also have significant shore bombardment and anti-air warfare capabilities. They are 560 feet long, with a beam of 54 feet. The armament includes missiles, a 5-inch gun, and anti-submarine rockets. The crew consists of 270 officers and men. The first major U.S. Navy ships to be powered by gas turbines, (the four marine gas turbines generate 80,000 horsepower), these ships have a rated speed in excess of 30 knots. *Spruance* class ships have controllable, reversible pitch propellers, giving them a high degree of maneuverability.

U.S.S. KIDD (DDG-993)

The *Kidd* class of four ships, which were originally ordered by the Iranian government in 1974, is a variation of the *Spruance* class design. These ships are optimized for general warfare instead of the anti-submarine warfare specialty of the *Spruance* class. As a result, their displacement is 8,500 tons; however, their other characteristics are the same as the *Spruance*. They were commissioned in the U.S. Navy in 1981 and 1982, and are the most powerful destroyers in the Fleet.

U.S.S. BROOKE (FFG-1)

Lead ship of a class of six guided missile frigates, *Brooke* was commissioned in 1966. Originally known as Destroyer Escort (DE) types, they were reclassified as Frigates in 1975. Size and design are similar to that of the *Garcia* class of FF; however, addition of a guided missile battery strengthen their role of AAW escort. *Brooke* carries a Tartar missile battery in lieu of the after 5-inch gun of the *Garcia* class, and retains the forward 5-incher. She also retains the ASROC and DASH installa-

U.S.S. *Kidd*

tions, giving her a strong ASW capability. *Brooke* class ships, like *Garcia* and *Knox* classes, carry crews of approximately 200 officers and men. All have rated speeds of about 27 knots.

U.S.S. KNOX (FF-1052)

The most modern and largest of the FF types, *Knox* is lead ship of the class of 46 ships. Displacing 4,100 tons, full load, with a length of 438 feet, these ships are the equivalent of modern destroyers in all respects except speed and firepower. Their two boilers generate about 35,000 horsepower, giving a rated speed of about 27 knots. The ships of this class have a massive bow-mounted SONAR projecting beneath the bow.

U.S.S. *Brooke*

U.S.S. Knox

U.S.S. GARCIA (FF-1040)   Commissioned in 1964 as a DE, this is the first of the 10-ship *Garcia* class of modern, large escorts that were reclassified as Frigates in 1975. These ships are 414½ feet long, and displace 3,400 tons. Their rated 27-knot speed allows them to escort high-speed convoys and task forces, as well as equipping them well for the speed necessary to track fast-moving submarines. Their armament consists of two 5-inch guns, ASROC, and DASH; their SONAR assists in the detection and tracking of enemy submarines.

51

U.S.S. *Garcia*

1040

U.S.S. COPELAND (FFG-25)

One of the *Oliver Hazard Perry* (FFG-7) class of guided missile frigates. The *Perry* class is a new design capable of operating against air, surface, and subsurface threats. A total of 60 ships of this class will be built. These ships displace 3,600 tons, full load, and are 445 feet in length, with a beam of 45 feet and a draft of 24 feet. Powered by two gas turbines, which can develop 40,000 shaft horsepower, they have a speed of 30 knots. They have Harpoon and Standard missiles, and are capable of firing Tomahawk missiles as well. In addition, they have hull-mounted SONAR and a towed array for detection of submarines, two LAMPS helicopters, and two triple torpedo tubes.

U.S.S. *Copeland*

Part 4 — SUBMARINES

Submarines have long played an important part in warfare at sea. From their earliest uses for patrol and scouting, planting "mines" and explosive charges, and attacking enemy shipping, they have relied primarily upon their ability to stay hidden beneath the surface—and that is still one of their most important assets.

The addition of nuclear power has greatly increased the importance of submarines, for now they are true submersibles which can stay under the ocean for weeks or months and can cruise at great speeds while submerged. Both of these, long submergence and great submerged speed, are capabilities that were not possible when submarines relied upon diesel engines, requiring air and fuel, and electric storage batteries, requiring frequent recharging. Since they can be designed for almost unlimited submerged operations, nuclear-powered boats can have hull forms especially adapted to higher submerged speeds than are possible on the surface.

The use of atomic fuel gives a submarine almost unlimited cruising range at top speed without the need for frequent refueling. Some strategists believe that future navies may be largely submarine-type ships, retaining their original missions, but relying on staying submerged to protect them from enemy missiles.

Today's Navy submarines have a number of missions. They perform tactical functions of patrol, reconnaissance, attacking enemy shipping, and detecting and attacking enemy submarines. They are also frequently used as radar picket stations in locations near enemy coastlines, and as rescue stations for downed aircraft crews just off enemy coasts.

In addition, the Fleet Ballistic Missile (FBM) submarines perform the role of strategic deterrence. The U.S. Navy has 34 active SSBNs, armed with Poseidon or Trident missiles, and eleven more are planned for the future. These submarines can remain submerged and hidden from detection in ocean waters well within range of any potential enemy's important targets. The fact that the U.S. Navy has this capability is a strong deterrent against an enemy who may attempt to start a surprise war, hoping to knock out all U.S. offensive weapons in the first attack. Thus, the hidden SSBNs, armed with powerful missiles with nuclear warheads, are an important

U.S.S. *Lafayette*

U.S.S. Ohio

U.S. weapon for the prevention of future wars. A number of SSBNs are kept on station at all times, cruising deep in the oceans of the world, ready to retaliate for any enemy attack against the United States.

U.S.S. LAFAYETTE (SSBN-616)   The *Lafayette* class originally was 31 ships; however, two new variations have been made which divide the 31 into three distinct classes: *Lafayette* class of 9 ships, *James Madison* (SSBN-627) class of 10 ships, and the *Benjamin Franklin* (SSBN-640) class of 12 ships. They are distinguished by slightly different configurations and by the addition of Trident C-4 conversions on the two new classes. All displace 8,250 tons and are capable of speeds in excess of 20 knots submerged. Their length is 425 feet, beam is 33 feet, and draft when surfaced is 28 feet. The nuclear reactor core elements in these submarines provide energy for approximately 400,000 miles of travel.

U.S.S. OHIO (SSBN-726)   This is the lead ship of a new class of highly survivable ballistic missile-carrying submarines. Seventeen of this class are planned. Each carries 24 Trident missiles, capable of striking targets as far as 4,000 miles from the launch point. These are by far the largest submarines in the U.S. Navy. They displace 18,700 tons, and are 560 feet in length, with a beam of 42 feet and a draft of 36 feet.

U.S.S. LOS ANGELES (SSN-688)   The *Los Angeles* class of nuclear attack submarines is the newest of several classes of these important elements of our Navy's undersea forces charged with control of the seas. Their mission, as for all SSNs, is to destroy enemy ships, primarily submarines, in order to prevent their use for attack and destruction of U.S. or allied targets. This class, to consist of 54 ships, is named after cities of the U.S. They are characterized by high submerged speed, improved sensors and weapons, and maximum quietness. *Los Angeles* class submarines have a length of 360 feet, a beam of 33 feet, and a displacement of 6,900 tons.

U.S.S. ASPRO (SSN-648)   This submarine is a member of the *Sturgeon* (SSN-637) class. The most numerous attack submarine class, with 37 ships in service, the *Sturgeon* class submarines are very capable members of the Navy's submarine forces. Similar to the *Los Angeles* class, but older, smaller, and lacking the submerged

U.S.S. *Sturgeon*

U.S.S. *Los Angeles*

U.S.S. *Aspro*

of the newer design, the ships of the *Sturgeon* class still are able to hold their own in the mission of sea control. Ships of this class have a length of 292 feet, and a beam of 33 feet. They displace 4,640 tons.

U.S.S. PERMIT (SSN-594)   The *Permit* (photograph on page 12) is the lead ship of the 13-ship class formerly known as the *Thresher* class. They are one of the Navy's prime anti-submarine weapon systems, and are extremely quiet and maneuverable, with a full array of sensors and weapons for the destruction of enemy submarines. These ships have a length of 279 feet and displace 4,300 tons.

Part 5 — AMPHIBIOUS WARFARE SHIPS

The U.S. Navy developed the techniques of modern amphibious warfare in World War II, and has been improving upon them in the years since. To take and hold territory requires that our troops be put on enemy-held shores, equipped to overcome enemy troops and to sustain operations for an indefinite period. The role of the Navy is to transport our troops and their equipment from their bases to the enemy shores, and to land them safely and efficiently. To do so requires a number of different types of ships— each with its own part to play as a member of the Navy amphibious warfare team.

New ships, with greater carrying capacity and greater speed, have been developed for modern amphibious warfare. The advent of the helicopter has played an important part in landing troops ashore. Helicopters allow rapid transport of the first wave of soldiers or Marines from the large ships which brought them to the battle area. Landing behind the enemy lines, they can quickly establish a beachhead for the waves of assault boats carrying heavy support equipment and other troops. Such new tactics require new types of ships; these have been developed to enhance our Navy's amphibious warfare capabilities.

The primary mission of the amphibious force is to land troops on enemy-controlled territory. Using command ships (LCC) to direct and control landings, assault ships (LHA and LPH), transports (LPD), and cargo ships (LKA) to carry troops and equipment, tank landing ships (LST) to transport the heavy tanks and trucks to the beach, and a variety of support ships of different types, the Navy has become adept at carrying out this mission. The amphibious ships are well supported by gunfire and missiles from escorting cruisers and destroyers, and by bombing and strafing by aircraft from nearby carriers. They are provided air defense and defense against submarines by units of supporting task forces.

U.S.S. IWO JIMA (LPH-2)
The LPH is a relatively new type of amphibious ship, one designed to carry helicopters and troops for making airborne assaults on or behind beachheads. *Iwo Jima* is the lead ship of a seven-ship class of LPH. Commissioned in 1961, she normally carries about 2,000 troops and from 20 to 30 assault helicopters, and can proceed to assault areas at speeds as high as her rated top of 20

U.S.S. *Iwo Jima*

U.S.S. *Blue Ridge*

The amphibious transport dock U.S.S. *Coronado* (LPD-11), the tank landing ship U.S.S. *Suffolk County* (LST-1173), and the amphibious assault ship U.S.S. *Inchon* (LPH-12) cruise in formation.

knots. The *Iwo Jima* class ships displace 18,000 tons, and are 592 feet long, with a 105-foot beam, and 26-foot draft. They are known as Amphibious Assault Ships.

U.S.S. BLUE RIDGE (LCC-19)

Two modern Amphibious Command Ships, *Blue Ridge* and her sister ship, *Mount Whitney* (LCC-20), are used as the command headquarters for amphibious operations. Located aboard these ships are the commanders of both the ship forces and the landing forces involved in the amphibious assaults. These Navy Admirals and Army and Marine Corps Generals and their staffs plan, direct, and control the landing operations from the command ships. The ships have adequate space for the staffs and for plotting the positions of their forces, allowing constant monitoring and control of their operations. They also have the necessary communications facilities for maintaining radio contact with a large number

U.S.S. *Tarawa*

of units, both at sea and ashore. These ships displace 19,000 tons, are 620 feet long, and have a beam of 108 feet. Designed for a speed of 20 knots, they are able to stay in the forefront of modern amphibious task forces.

U.S.S. TARAWA (LHA-1)

Tarawa is the first of five ships in a new class of amphibious assault ships. She is the largest amphibious ship in service, able to embark, deploy, and land a fully equipped Marine assault force by helicopter and landing craft. A single LHA-1 class ship can perform many of the functions which previously required four different types of amphibious ships. *Tarawa* is 820 feet in length, with a beam of 106 feet, and a displacement of 39,300 tons, fully loaded. She is capable of speeds in excess of 20 knots, and carries more than 2,700 men, including her own officers and men and the embarked Marines.

U.S.S. CHARLESTON (LKA-113) The LKA types are Attack Cargo Ships which carry the necessary "assault loaded combat cargo" for amphibious landings. The most vital cargo (food, guns, ammunition, clothing, medical supplies, etc.) is stowed near the top of the holds so as to be sent to the beachhead with the first assault waves, followed by the cargo necessary to sustain an operation after the beachhead is secured. Most are converted merchant cargo ships; the *Charleston* class of 5 ships is the first built from keel up as LKAs. They displace 20,000 tons, are 550 feet long, and have a rated top speed of 20 knots. They carry as many as 24 landing craft (assault boats) to offload the cargo and ferry it in to the beaches when needed. The many booms on the decks are for offloading the boats and then lifting the heavy cargo from deep in the holds of the ship into the boats.

U.S.S. *Charleston*

U.S.S. *Mount Vernon*

U.S.S. MOUNT VERNON (LSD-39)

The Dock Landing Ship is built around a drydocklike well which may be flooded or drained dry as desired. Thus, the ship may be used as a drydock for small ships and boats—or, as more often happens, she may carry fully loaded landing craft in the dry well. When in the landing area, she floods the dock and opens the stern gate, allowing the craft to become waterborne and depart rapidly for the beach. *Mount Vernon* is a member of the five-ship *Anchorage* (LSD-36) class. She carries a crew of about 300 and has cranes capable of lifting 50 tons—important assets to her drydock work and assault craft loading. She may carry as many as 21 assault boats.

U.S.S. AUSTIN (LPD-4) *Austin* is the lead ship of a class of 12 Amphibious Transport, Dock ships. The LPD ships combine the functions of Amphibious Transport (LPA), Dock Landing Ship (LSD), and Amphibious Assault (LPH) ships. The *Austin* class ships all displace 17,150 tons when fully loaded, are 581 feet long, and are capable of speeds of 21 knots, allowing them to make fast approaches to the assault area. These ships, like the LSD types, can launch preloaded landing craft from the well deck in the stern. The platform above the well deck is the landing pad for helicopters which may be used to take combat forces ashore, in the style of the LPH ships. *Austin* class ships can carry over a thousand troops and all of their equipment for an assault landing.

U.S.S. *Austin*

U.S.S. *Newport*

U.S.S. NEWPORT (LST-1179)   The lead ship of an 18-ship class of new design LSTs, *Newport* displaces 8,400 tons, has an overall length of 517 feet, a beam of 68 feet, and a rated speed of 20 knots. These are the largest and fastest LSTs ever built, with modern equipment and a bow ramp instead of the bow doors of previous classes of LSTs. The LST types, originally developed in World War II, revolutionized amphibious warfare by their ability to drive their flat-bottomed bows high up on a beach, drop their ramps on dry land, and off-load great numbers of tanks, trucks, and equipment of all kinds. The main load is prepacked trucks with their cargo for combat in place when they are driven on the ships. Heavy tanks and armored vehicles are also carried in this way. The displacement of these LSTs is normally 20 feet; however, when a landing is planned, the ballast is shifted (usually by pumping fuel and water from forward compartments to after ones) so that the forward draft is decreased to 3 or 4 feet, thus making possible a "dry ramp" landing when the bow is beached.

Part 6 — ESCORT, PATROL, AND MINE WARFARE SHIPS

In wartime the Navy needs many maneuverable, hard-working ships to perform the functions of escorting and patrolling. It must be prepared to furnish escorts to large numbers of merchant vessels without the ability to defend themselves—they depend upon their Navy escorts for protection against enemy surface ships, submarines, and aircraft. During World War II many merchant convoys were shepherded safely through submarine-infested waters by the nimble, fast escort ships of the Navy—many of which were converted to escort types from other ship designs.

Similar fast, maneuverable ships are used for patrolling and protecting coasts and harbors in friendly territory, or for blockading enemy areas to prevent entry from the sea. In Vietnam, Navy patrols were extended to the many rivers and inlets of that country, and the patrol vessels of importance for those operations were the speedy, heavily armed Patrol Gunboats (PG) and the Inshore Patrol Craft (PCF), better known as "Swift Boats." These types were especially developed and equipped for riverine patrol duty.

Mine warfare ships have characteristics similar to those of escort and patrol vessels. In addition, they have been designed to detect, dislodge, and destroy mines which have been placed in waters where our ships must operate. When not used for mine hunting, the minesweepers may also be used for patrol and escort duties.

The primary mission of all of these versatile ships is one of protection of our larger ships and forces. They are designed for and adapted to the protective role—protection of our ships from enemy sea forces, and protection of our troops ashore from infiltration by enemy troops from the sea and river approaches. The protection against mines is a valuable function—especially for those ships engaged in amphibious operations or other such actions which bring them into shallow waters where mines may have been planted.

The primary escort ships are the Frigates (FF)—originally called Destroyer Escorts (DE). They are a departure from the rule that most of the escorts are small and light. Modern FF types are large and complex; they resemble the DD types of prior years, hence are illustrated in Part 3—Destroyers and Frigates. In appearance, they look like Destroyers but generally are less heavily armed, specializing in the weapons used for ASW (Anti-Submarine Warfare) and AAW (Anti-Aircraft Warfare). They carry the most

U.S.S. *Leader*

modern SONAR (SOund Navigation And Ranging) equipment for the location and tracking of submerged submarines, and modern weapons such as ASROC (Anti-Submarine Rockets) and DASH (Drone Anti-Submarine Helicopter) for attacking and destroying enemy subs.

U.S.S. LEADER (MSO-490)

A non-magnetic Ocean Minesweeper (MSO) in the *Aggressive* (MSO-422) class, *Leader* is one of a class of 26 in the U.S. Navy, of which only three remain in active service—U.S.S. *Fidelity* (MSO-443), and U.S.S. *Illusive* (MSO-448) are the other two. A number of additional ships of the same design have been sold to other friendly nations. These ships are 172 feet long, have crews of 72 officers and men, and displace 760 tons. Their two diesel engines give them a rated speed of 15 knots. These non-magnetic ships have plywood hulls, diesel engines built with special non-magnetic stainless steel alloys, and other metal fittings made of aluminum or brass—all to make the ship as resistant as possible to the magnetic influence mines which they may be called upon to sweep. Each minesweeper has long "tails" which are unrolled and towed astern to destroy magnetic mines. The "tails" are heavy electric cables which, connected to gas turbine-driven electric generators, put large electric currents in the water astern of the ship, creating magnetic fields well away from the ship. These fields set off the magnetic mines and destroy them when they are safely astern and away from the ship. The reason for keeping the ships as non-magnetic as possible is to avoid setting off the mines prematurely. The MSO ships are also equipped to sweep (dislodge or detonate) mines of the acoustic or contact type.

U.S.S. MARATHON (PG-89)

The Patrol Gunboat (PG) class came into prominence in the Vietnam War, where its powerful firepower and close-in support of shore forces, as well as its speed and maneuverability were perfect for the type of operations conducted there. *Marathon* was commissioned in 1968, the sixth of the seventeen-ship *Asheville* (PG-84) class. All have aluminum hulls and fiberglass superstructures. They are 165 feet long and carry a 3-inch gun forward—the largest gun ever mounted on a ship of that size. They also carry 40-millimeter cannon and 50-caliber machine guns. The mission of the PG is to blockade coastal shipping and defend amphibious forces; since the forward 3-inch gun can accurately place fifty 13-pound projectiles a minute in a target area, their firepower is respected by enemies and ad-

U.S.S. *Marathon*

mired by friendly forces. Main engine of each PG is a 14,000 horsepower J79 gas turbine, similar to those found in high-performance jet aircraft. *Marathon* can go from a standing start to 40 knots in less than a minute. Twin diesels provide power for low-speed, high-endurance cruising.

U.S.S. *Pegasus*

U.S.S. PEGASUS (PHM-1)   The lead ship of six operational PHM (Patrol Hydrofoil, Missile) ships of the *Pegasus* class, this is a 235-ton design—the U.S. Navy's largest operational hydrofoil. These ships are a joint venture of the U.S. Navy and two North Atlantic Treaty Organization allies, Italy and West Germany. Hydrofoil ships are designed to "fly" on their hydrofoils at speeds in excess of 40 knots. Such high speeds are especially beneficial when the ships are engaged in chase or rescue operations. Ships equipped with hydrofoils will normally cruise with their foils retracted. When high speeds are required, they will lower their foils in the water and increase their engine speeds. The foils will exert force against the water and provide lift, raising the hull higher, decreasing the drag, thus allowing for still greater speed. As speed increases, the lift increases, until the entire hull is clear of the water, and the ship "flies" on her foils alone. During wartime, the ships will be used to detect and attack enemy forces. The ability to deliver missiles while flying at speeds of more than 40 knots—in virtually any sea state—is expected to provide a needed asset to our naval forces. *Pegasus* has a hull of welded aluminum alloy; struts and foils are stainless steel. Her length is 131.2 feet (40 meters), beam is 28.2 feet (8.6 meters), and draft with foils retracted is 6.2 feet (1.9 meters). When foilborne, her draft is about 8.8 feet (2.7 meters). Propulsion when hullborne is provided by two diesel engines which power two steerable waterjet propulsors. When foilborne, propulsion is provided by a single waterjet pump system, driven by a gas turbine engine. *Pegasus* is armed with a 76 mm gun and Harpoon missiles. She was designed and built by the Boeing Aerospace Company and was launched in November, 1974. Her crew consists of 4 officers and 17 enlisted men.

Part 7 — AUXILIARY SHIPS AND UNDERWAY REPLENISHMENT SHIPS

It has been said that the Navy could enter a war without its Underway Replenishment Ships, but it couldn't keep up the fight for very long. These are the ships that replenish the stores, fuel, food, ammunition, and repair parts that are used by the combatant ships during their operations. They may be likened to "the man behind the man behind the gun," although they are frequently so near the actual fighting that they, too, are a part of it.

A Navy needs a variety of ships not designed for combat, but essential to keep the combatant types supplied and repaired. There are as many types of such auxiliary ships as there are jobs to be done. The tenders, for example, carry repair parts and have workshops for all types of repairs. They are "mother ships" for the ships assigned to their care, providing all of the essentials for forward area support. Destroyer Tenders (AD), Submarine Tenders (AS), and Salvage Ships (ARS) are perhaps the most important auxiliary types; they follow the Fleet and provide the "Can do" answer of skilled craftsmen. Repair ships (AR) are similar to tenders, but their work is not limited to any particular type of ship.

Supply ships of all types are also part of the auxiliary fleet. Combat Stores Ships (AFS), Oilers (AO), Ammunition Ships (AE), as well as combinations of these such as Fast Combat Support Ships (AOE) and Replenishment Oilers (AOR), carry the food, fuel, and ammunition needed by the ships being supported. As soon as one of the Underway Replenishment Ships issues all of its material, it returns to base to take on another load; meanwhile, its place in the supply force has been taken by another with a full load of vital cargo.

There are many other auxiliaries—rescue ships, research ships, tugs, and other specialized types—as many as are needed to keep a fighting fleet in fighting trim.

U.S.S. BRYCE CANYON (AD-36)

One of nine ships built from modified C3 merchant types during World War II, *Bryce Canyon* carries a crew of skilled craftsmen to man the ship and her shops. These Destroyer Tenders serve as floating service stations for the many Destroyers under their care. They are

U.S.S. Bryce Canyon

U.S.S. *Holland*

large ships—displacing 16,635 tons, and having an overall length of 492 feet. Their main engines generate 8,500 horsepower, enough to drive the ships at a rated speed of 18.4 knots.

U.S.S. HOLLAND (AS-32)   The Submarine Tenders are similar to the ADs except for their special shops and skills devoted to the needs of submarines and their crews. *Holland* is of the recently built *Hunley* class (AS-31), and was commissioned in 1963. These are FBM Submarine Tenders, with the handling and storage equipment as well as the workshops and trained men for servicing the Polaris missiles. These tenders displace 18,300 tons and are 599 feet long. Their main engines are diesels, capable of generating 15,000 horsepower to drive the ships at rated speeds of 18 knots.

U.S.S. *Vulcan*

U.S.S. Papago

U.S.S. VULCAN (AR-5)   *Vulcan* is the lead ship of four sister-ships of the class. These are pre-World War II ships, built between 1938 and 1941. They are 529 feet long, displace 16,200 tons, and have rated speeds of 19.2 knots. They specialize in repair work for all types of ships in the Fleet and may frequently be found in forward areas providing excellent repair service to nearby ships. They carry a crew of 1,100 men, many of them skilled in repair work of different kinds. These auxiliaries are built to fight when necessary—each ship carries four 5-inch guns.

U.S.S. PAPAGO (ATF-160) and U.S.S. EDENTON (ATS-1)   These are a fleet tug and a salvage tug, of which there are a number of different types and classes, with slightly different arrangements and displace-

U.S.S. *Edenton*

U.S.S. Vega

ments. They are powerful little ships that are called upon for salvage and towing work, and they do an excellent job under sometimes trying conditions. Their powerful diesel engines can tow much larger ships off reefs and beaches; they have been known to tow battle-damaged ships thousands of miles to shipyards where the damage could be repaired. Ships of the ATS type are expected to replace the older ATFs in the future.

U.S.S. VEGA (AF-59)   A refrigerated stores ship, *Vega* is one of the two-ship *Rigel* class. Both ships were built in the mid-1950's from Maritime Administration design adapted to Navy uses. They can follow the Fleet at speeds of 21 knots, keeping up with all but the fastest-moving task forces, ready to provide the fresh and frozen products needed for healthy and happy crews. These ships are 502 feet long and displace 15,450 tons.

U.S.S. Pyro

U.S.S. *Hassayampa*

U.S.S. PYRO (AE-24)   *Pyro* is an ammunition ship of the five-ship *Suribachi* class. Commissioned in 1959, she is 502 feet long and displaces 17,400 tons with a full load. All of this class have new handling equipment for carrying and transferring guided missiles to the ships using them. They have a rated top speed of 21 knots.

U.S.S. HASSAYAMPA (AO-145)   This ship is one of the modern *Neosho* class Fleet Oilers used for underway replenishment of the fuel of those ships that burn oil. There are six sister-ships in this class (AO-143 through AO-148), all built in the 1950 era to the same design. They are 655 feet long, displace 38,000 tons, and have a maximum draft of 35 feet. Their steam turbine main engines produce 28,000 horsepower to drive them at rated speeds of 20 knots. Manned by a crew of 324 officers and men, these ships can each carry 180,000 barrels of fuel oil as cargo.

U.S.S. SACRAMENTO (AOE-1)   This is the largest of the auxiliaries: 793 feet long, 39 foot draft, 53,000 tons displacement. Commissioned in 1964, *Sacramento* is the lead ship of a new class which combines the functions of Oiler (AO), Ammunition Ship (AE), and Stores Cargo Ship (AF/AK). She carries 177,000 barrels of oil and aviation fuel, ammunition, and missiles as large as the Talos size. Her two steam turbine main engines produce sufficient power (estimated at 100,000 horsepower) to drive her enormous hull through the water at 26 knots.

U.S.S. *Sacramento*

Part 8 — SHIPS OF THE FUTURE

Ship designs change as the years go by. Our Navy is constantly looking ahead and designing new ships which will perform their future missions more effectively and more efficiently, no matter what those missions may be. The objectives of new designs are to replace older, obsolete ships and to increase the readiness and effectiveness of the U.S. Navy.

Some new designs are the result of changes in the technology and techniques of warfare. The guided missile ships and the nuclear-powered ships in today's Navy are examples of advancing technology resulting in new ship designs. In earlier years, the development of aircraft led to ships designed to be "aircraft carriers"—as a result, our Fleets of today are strongly oriented toward our carriers and their aircraft.

Some new designs result from changes in mission. The Fleet Ballistic Missile submarine developed from the need for the Navy to assume a new role—that of strategic force for the prevention of enemy attacks. Thus a new mission—strategic deterrent—resulted in perfection of a new type of ship.

Some new designs are developed to combine the missions of several ships into a single hull. The AOE, for example, provides to the operating forces a capability of Oiler, Stores ship, and Ammunition ship all in the same hull.

Finally, some designs are developed simply to take advantage of improvements in certain types of ships, and to improve the new model so it can do the same job better than previous classes.

All of these design changes are important. Whether they will survive through the years or will, in turn, be replaced by still later improvements remains to be seen. Looking ahead, one may visualize the Navy of the future by some of the new ship designs now on the drawing boards and in the minds of the designers. Some of those are shown here. Many of these designs will never be built—they are conceptual; they represent ideas only. Some will be built; others are now being built. These are the artists' conceptions of new designs.

U.S.S. ARLEIGH BURKE (DDG-51)
This is an artist's concept of the lead ship of a new class of guided missile destroyers to be named after Admiral Arleigh Burke, one of the Navy's most famous Destroyermen of

U.S.S. Arleigh Burke (drawing)

World War II and later years. He was the Chief of Naval Operations from 1955 to 1961, and it is most fitting that this new class of ships is to be named to honor him. These 8,500-ton-displacement ships are intended to complement the CG-47 class in providing Aegis fleet air defense capability.

SURFACE EFFECT SHIP (SES)

This is a revolutionary type of warship that is expected to be able to race across oceans on a bubble of air at 100 miles per hour. Two test craft have been built and tested. They are 100-ton craft, 80-feet long, with a beam of 40 feet, and have reached speeds of greater than 80 miles per hour. A large prototype warship is planned, displacing about 3,000 tons, 275 feet long, beam of 105 feet, and powered by six gas turbines. The SES is a variation of the air cushion vehicle, using rigid sidewalls

Below: **Design submitted for the prototype of the 3,000-ton Surface Effect Ship.** *Opposite:* **Artist's concept of a Small Waterplane Area Twin Hull ship.**

to contain the "bubble" of air on which it rides. Powerful fans create a cushion of air which raises the ship above the surface, leaving only the sidewalls and flexible seals fore and aft touching the surface and holding the air bubble. The drag and wave friction is reduced considerably, allowing the SES to move at high speeds. The Navy plans to use SES type ships for anti-submarine warfare missions. They are also well suited for search-and-rescue and coastal patrol missions.

SWATH SHIP   SWATH stands for Small Waterplane Area Twin Hull, and it describes a ship that appears to be connected by struts to two submerged submarine hulls. This design provides a very stable, smooth-riding ship that can perform a number of important missions for the Navy. Speeds of 35 to 40 knots are possible with this type of ship, and the increased deck space made possible by the catamaran-like construction would be excellent for aircraft or helicopter platforms. At present, only a small (190-ton) semi-submerged platform (SSP), the *Kaimalino,* has been built to test the design. It has been shown to be a very stable, versatile design which will probably find a useful role in future Navy operations.

SWATH SHIP AIRCRAFT CARRIER   One possible use of the SWATH ship design is for future aircraft carriers, perhaps similar to the conceptual design shown here. The stability and speed of this ship design, combined with the large deck space available for a flight deck, make the design ideal for small carriers which could carry new concept VATOL (Vertical Assist Takeoff and Landing) aircraft.

AIR CAPABLE SHIP   Another conceptual design for a possible new type of aircraft carrier is shown on the following page. The Air Capable Ship would have a number of possible uses, but the most obvious one would be that of a small aircraft carrier. This artist's drawing is only one of a number of possible configurations. This one is built on catamaran hulls—that is, two individual hulls with open water in between and a large flight deck built atop both hulls.

Note that this is not the same as a SWATH design because the two hulls are essentially two smaller ship hulls, not a small waterplane design as pictured on page 91 in which most of the hulls are submerged and only a small vertical structure is at the surface.

Kaimalino (SSP) underway with an H-2 Seasprite helicopter landing on the deck.

Below: Artist's concept of SWATH ship design for aircraft carrier.

Artist's conceptual design for an Air Capable Ship.

INDEX